The Bell Family in Baddeck

Alexander Graham Bell and Mabel Bell in Cape Breton

Judith Tulloch

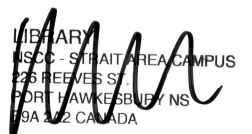
Formac Publishing Company Limited
Halifax

Formac Publishing Company Limited recognizes the support of the Province of Nova Scotia through the Department of Tourism, Culture and Heritage. We acknowledge the financial support of the Government of Canada through the Book Publishing Industry Development Program (BPIDP) for our publishing activities. Formac Publishing Company Limited acknowledges the support of the Canada Council for the Arts for our publishing program.

The Canada Council | Le Conseil des Arts
for the Arts | du Canada

NOVA SCOTIA
Tourism, Culture and Heritage

Library and Archives Canada Cataloguing in Publication

Tulloch, Judith
        The Bell family in Baddeck : Alexander Graham Bell and
        Mabel Bell in Cape Breton / Judith Tulloch.

Includes bibliographical references and index.
ISBN-13: 978-0-88780-713-8
ISBN-10: 0-88780-713-5

        1. Bell, Alexander Graham, 1847-1922. 2. Bell, Mabel
Gardiner Hubbard, 1859-1923. 3. Baddeck (N.S.)—Biography.
4. Inventors—Canada—Biography. 5. Inventors—United States—
Biography.
I. Title.

TK6143.B4T84 2006   621.385092   C2006-903305-6

Formac Publishing Company Limited
5502 Atlantic Street
Halifax, Nova Scotia
B3H 1G4
www.formac.ca

Printed and bound in Canada

Contents

Preface

For more than 30 years, Alexander Graham Bell and his family made their summer home at Beinn Bhreagh, near Baddeck, Nova Scotia. There Alec conducted experiments in areas as diverse as aviation and genetics. His children and grandchildren swam, sailed and hiked, enjoying all the pleasures of summer in the country.

Photography was an important part of life at Beinn Bhreagh. Gilbert Grosvenor, husband of the Bells' elder daughter Elsie, recorded the activities of friends and family as well as the special events that highlighted the seasons. Photographs also documented the progress of Alec's experiments. He insisted that his workmen date the photos so that they could be used in court cases, a lesson he had learned from the legal challenges to his telephone patent.

I have drawn on the vast photograph collection that accumulated to illustrate both the scientific achievements of Alec's work and the loving family life that Mabel Bell cherished. The images that form the basis of this book evoke the full breadth of life at Beinn Bhreagh a century ago.

— J.T.

The Bell home at Brantford: Alexander Graham Bell and his daughter Elsie visit in 1906.

Introduction

In August 1870, the Scottish educator Alexander
Melville Bell, his wife Eliza and their 23-year-old son
Alexander Graham, recent immigrants to Canada,
settled into their new home in Tutelo Heights (now
called Tutela Heights), Ontario. It was a comfortable
roomy house, set in the southern Ontario countryside only a few miles from the busy industrial town
of Brantford. For the Bell family, it represented the
start of a new life.

They had lived for many years in Edinburgh where

Three generations of Alexander Bells: (l. to r.) Alexander Melville, Alec and grandfather Alexander.

Alexander Melville taught speech and elocution and lectured regularly at the University of Edinburgh. He had gained fame as the inventor of a system of symbols representing vocal sounds, a system that he named "Visible Speech." Alexander Melville and Eliza's three sons, Melville, Alexander and Edward, all born in the mid-1840s, were active curious boys who delighted in music and loved to ramble in the Scottish countryside when they stayed at the family's rural cottage near Edinburgh.

As young boys, the Bell sons were educated at home by their mother and in time went on to the Royal High School, where generations of Edinburgh boys had studied. Melly did well at school, younger brothers Alec and Ted less well. In 1862, the 15-year-old Alec was sent to London to live with his grandfather, another Alexander Bell who taught speech and elocution. Grandfather Bell tutored him in English literature and language so successfully that a year later Alec obtained a post teaching music and elocution at Weston, a private boys' school in northern Scotland. He taught for a year while Melly attended classes at the University of Edinburgh and then the two exchanged places. Ted also planned to teach at Weston in his turn.

The brothers seemed destined for a life of teaching and writing. Then in the autumn of 1866 Ted fell ill with tuberculosis. A winter of rest did nothing to stop the disease and in May he died peacefully in his sleep at the age of 18. Alec moved to London to live with his parents and study at University College, while Melly remained in Edinburgh, carrying on the Bell tradition of teaching speech and elocution. But three years later,

Alec's mother, Eliza Grace Bell.

Alec (top row right) with staff and students at the Boston School for the Deaf in 1871.

Melly too was dead of tuberculosis, the disease that caused so much sorrow in Victorian families at all levels of society. Only Alec remained. His worried parents watched their thin pale son and were determined to safeguard him. Alexander Melville, remembering how the clear air of Newfoundland had restored his own health years before, decided that the family should emigrate to Canada. Reluctantly, Alec agreed, saddened to leave the life of study and teaching he had contemplated for himself but unable to cause his parents more grief than they had already experienced. Arrangements were quickly made and the family sailed from England on July 21, 1870.

The first months at Tutela Heights passed easily. Alec spent lazy days stretched out on the bluff overlooking Brantford resting and reading. As he grew stronger, he began to look for more challenging activities. When his father turned down the chance to teach speech at a school for deaf children in Boston, Alec leapt at it and by early spring 1871 was off on a new adventure.

Boston proved to be a congenial place with its fine public library, museums, universities and technical institutes. Alec entered fully into the intellectual life of the city, attending lectures on a myriad of topics and discussing scientific problems with professors at the city's universities. He also began experiments in telecommunications with the idea of developing a multiple telegraph: a way to transmit more than one message at a time over a telegraph wire.

In the midst of all this activity, Alec continued to work with deaf children to improve their speech. One of his new pupils was 16-year-old Mabel Hubbard, who had lost her hearing at the age of five following a serious illness. Daughter of a well-to-do Boston family, Mabel was not impressed at first with her new tutor; but soon she was confiding to her mother that Alec had commented on the sweetness of her voice and in February she willingly struggled through Boston snowstorms to keep her appointments with him. As the months passed, Alec realized that he had fallen in love with his pupil, although he hid his feelings, concerned at the 10-year age difference between them. His restraint ended in the summer of 1875 when he told Mabel of his love for her. Perhaps somewhat overwhelmed, she replied that while she did not love him, she did not dislike him. With that encouragement, Alec was content. They were formally engaged later that fall,

The teenaged Mabel Hubbard studied in Germany before becoming Alec's pupil.

Gardiner Greene Hubbard and his wife Gertrude on the verandah of their Washington home.

on Mabel's 18th birthday.

Alec's busy life of teaching and lecturing continued, but increasingly he concentrated on his experiments with multiple telegraphy. Mabel's father, Gardiner Greene Hubbard, an entrepreneur characteristic of that expansive time, easily grasped the commercial value of the idea and provided financial support for Alec's work. Gradually, though, Alec came to realize that his experiments were leading toward electrical transmission of speech, rather than telegraphy. He and his young assistant Thomas Watson tried many combinations of receivers, transmitters and batteries as they worked busily in Alec's Boston workshop. Mabel's father urged Alec to complete the application to patent the concepts and, finally, on February 14, 1876, Hubbard filed what proved to be the vital document, prosaically entitled "Improvement to Telegraphy," with the American patent office.

Much remained to be worked out, but less than a month later Alec and Tom Watson were able to communicate between rooms of the Exeter Street workshop using the new device. Late in June 1876, Alec took his telephone equipment to Philadelphia to participate in the exposition celebrating the

American centennial, where eminent scientists, among them the Scottish physicist and university professor Sir William Thomson, tested the device and applauded its potential.

Buoyed by this success, Alec set off to Canada for a summer visit to his parents. The telephone equipment went with him and quickly became part of the family's social evenings. On August 3, Alec took his telephone receiver to the nearby village of Mount Pleasant. There he and local residents listened to songs and speeches by his father and uncle transmitted from the telegraph office in Brantford five miles away. A week later, he enjoyed greater success when he set up his equipment in the small town of Paris. Again family members and friends gathered in the telegraph office in Brantford and transmitted over the telegraph wires. For three hours, a group of fascinated townspeople listened through the scratchy interference while Alec's father, his uncle David and others performed eight miles away.

Back in Boston in the fall, Alec continued with demonstrations and tests. As the technological problems were being worked out, Gardiner Hubbard was determined to ensure the financial success of Alec's invention. In July 1877, the Bell Telephone Association

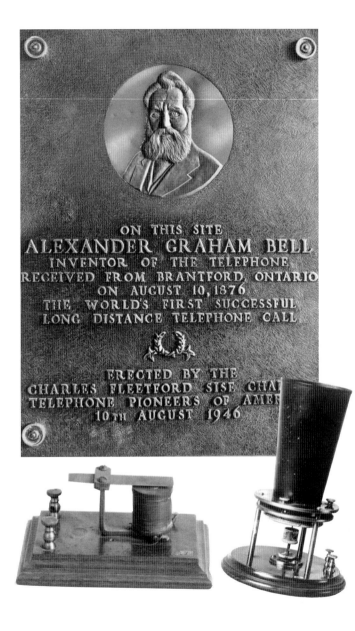

Top: Commemorative plaque at Paris, Ontario. Above: Model of the first working telephone.

Alec and Mabel at the time of their marriage.

was established, consisting of Hubbard, Alec, Tom Watson and Thomas Sanders, another early supporter of Alec's work. It was the beginning of financial security for all the partners and it freed Alec from the demands of the ordinary workplace forever.

More immediate concerns, however, were preoccupying the young inventor that summer. On July 11, after an engagement of 18 months, Mabel and Alec were married at the Hubbard home in Cambridge. They paid a short visit to Alec's family in Brantford, where the new bride was welcomed to the family with the Scottish tradition of having an oatcake broken over her head. Then they set off on an extended trip to Britain. By the time they returned to the United States in the autumn of 1878, the family had grown with the arrival of baby daughter Elsie May. Mabel's parents had decided to move to Washington and, on Mabel's urging, Alec agreed to join them. A second daughter Marian, known as Daisy, was born there in 1880. Alec found that life in Washington offered many opportunities. He set up a laboratory near his new home on Scott Circle and became acquainted with scientists and public men. Soon he was enjoying all the benefits of life in the

Invitation to Alec and Mabel's wedding, July 11, 1877.

The successful inventor at work in his new home in Washington.

Washington scientific establishment. Opportunities also arose from increasing prosperity. The Bells began to search for a summer home where they could experience the relaxed country life Alec had enjoyed as a boy. They found it by chance, on a summer trip to eastern Canada.

1 Hills, Lakes and Cool Climate

Baddeck in the 1880s was a small quiet village lying along the western shore of Bras d'Or Lake. It was the shire town for Victoria County, prosperous, already the subject of a travel book by the American writer Charles Dudley Warner, *Baddeck, and That Sort of Thing*. In August 1885, an American family from Washington—father, mother and two young daughters—arrived in the village, drawn by the vivid description of the community in Warner's book.

Alec's telephone patent, dated March 7, 1876: one of the most valuable patents ever issued.

The family was Alec, Mabel and daughters Elsie and Daisy. Their holiday in Baddeck that summer forged an enduring bond with Cape Breton.

By the mid-1880s, Alec was financially independent as a result of his invention of the telephone and his father-in-law's business skills. Although he continued to face challenges to his patent for many years, the economic success of the telephone company that took his name was assured. That success gave Alec and his family the freedom to travel widely and to devote themselves to an ever-widening range of interests.

In August 1885, Alec and Mabel had set off with Alexander Melville to travel through eastern Canada, spurred on by the elder Bell's desire to revisit St. John's, Newfoundland, where he had lived for a few years as a young man. Alec and Mabel for their part were eager to compare the reality of Baddeck with Warner's romantic description. After a brief stay in the village, the group continued on to Newfoundland; but when their ship was wrecked en route to St. John's, the Bells decided to return to Baddeck for a longer visit.

They stayed, as had Dudley Warner, at the Telegraph House, a white wooden building on the

main street with a view across the changeful waters of the lake towards a low headland known as Red Head. For several weeks during that sunny Cape Breton September, the Bells explored the countryside. They rowed and sailed on the lake, drove along the country roads enjoying restful views of lake, hills and glens, and luxuriated in the cool refreshing air, so different from the heat and humidity of Washington. The strong Scottish atmosphere of Cape Breton life, the customs and traditions of a population most of whom were descendants of settlers from Bell's homeland, made the area particularly inviting to him.

Baddeck, with Red Head in the background, at the time of the Bells' first visit.

By the end of their visit, Alec and Mabel had decided to return to Baddeck the next summer.

The Bells had been seeking the right place for a summer home for several years. They had visited the coasts of both Virginia and New England, but had not found the refuge they wanted. In an era before air-conditioning, many well-to-do families from large American and Canadian cities migrated every summer to cottages—some palatial, others more modest—in locations as diverse as Newport, Rhode Island; Bar Harbor, Maine; Murray Bay, Quebec; and, increasingly, the Canadian Maritime Provinces.

In July 1886, the family again made the long journey north by train, disembarking at Mulgrave on the Strait of Canso. The last stage of the trip was made by steamer, entering Bras d'Or Lake through the canal locks at St. Peter's and then sailing across the picturesque lake to Baddeck. This time the Bells stayed at a small cottage on the outskirts of Baddeck, rented for them by Arthur McCurdy, editor of the local newspaper, who had become a friend the previous summer. The Crescent Grove cottage was small and sparsely furnished. However, it gave the family the opportunity to experience the free and unconventional life that they wanted. Their daughters—eight-year-old Elsie

Mabel enjoying a quiet moment, far from the social obligations of Washington.

The family on holiday with Daisy (left) and Elsie (right) in boys' clothing.

and six-year-old Daisy—romped in the outdoors wearing the boys' clothing that Mabel had purchased for them, although she had preserved Victorian proprieties by pretending that the clothes were intended for boys who just happened to be the same size as her girls. Only in remote Baddeck was it possible for the girls to appear in boys' outfits. Mabel later reflected ironically that her granddaughters regularly wore clothing that their mothers had to travel a thousand miles to enjoy.

The cottage at Crescent Grove with a second storey added to house friends and family.

The days at Crescent Grove were agreeably busy. The family swam, boated and picked berries. Helped by Mabel's maid, they made attempts at rural domesticity, including making butter from the milk of the family cow. Churning, however, turned out to be much less entertaining than expected, and not even the encouragement of Alec's rousing version of *Onward Christian Soldiers* kept Mabel and her daughters from concluding that a mechanical churn would be a worthwhile addition to Alec's list of inventions.

One of the places Alec and Mabel explored that summer was Red Head, the headland on the other side of Baddeck Bay. From Crescent Grove they noticed how the afternoon sun flooded the meadow at the end of the point with light and warmth. One day they climbed to the top of the headland and admired the panoramic view of lake, islands and hills below them. They realized that this was the spot where they wanted to build a permanent summer home. It would be called Beinn Bhreagh: beautiful mountain.

The headland that they had fallen in love with was occupied by a number of farms and it took several years for Alec and Arthur McCurdy, now Alec's secretary, to persuade the farmers to part with their land. By 1888, Alec had acquired several hundred acres with a clear stream that provided a reliable water supply. At last, work began on the new home. Alec and Arthur drew up the plans together and Alec constructed a cardboard model to guide the carpenters.

When the family arrived in Baddeck in the summer of 1889, they found the house still under construction, but were so delighted with it that they moved in immediately. Their arrival however complicated the carpenters' workday since they now had to plan their tasks around the late-rising habits of the

View of Beinn Bhreagh in the early 1890s: the Bells' much-loved summer home.

23

The Lodge with the children's playhouse, Pansy Cottage, on the right.

family. Christened the Lodge, the house was a two-storey cottage with spacious living rooms on the ground floor and wide verandahs where family members and friends could relax and enjoy the scenic views. Other buildings were soon built nearby: a playhouse for Elsie, Daisy and their cousins, and a boathouse on the shore of the small harbour below the house. There was also a large laboratory where Alec could continue the experiments that occupied his wide-ranging mind.

Even as the Bells settled into the Lodge, they were already planning a larger home so that they could spend more time each year at Beinn Bhreagh. Comfortable as the Lodge was, it was still a summer home. Daisy Bell always remembered the cold when the family spent Christmas in Baddeck in 1890: "I remember the struggle it was for me to say goodnight to the group around the big fire downstairs and rush upstairs through the long dark cold corridor to my room. I must confess that I usually had a little fire of my own up there but it didn't do more than take the chill off the air although it did make lovely flickering patterns on the wall that I watched as long as I could keep my eyes open."

Mabel and Alec knew exactly where they wanted to build the new house: on the meadow at the western tip of the point where, Mabel said, "the sun's rays had full play from sunrise to sunset." Planning started in the summer of 1891. The Bells' coachman John MacDermid constructed a two-storey viewing platform on the farm wagon, Mabel and Alec took their places on the platform, and they drove slowly around the meadow looking for the spot that would give the best views for the new house.

Once they had settled on the location, they turned to the well-known Boston architects Cabot, Everett and Mead for the design. According to granddaughter

Alec and Mabel around the time of their arrival in Baddeck.

Lillian, "When the architect's drawings for the house came, Grandfather was in an autocratic mood quite rare for him, and he announced to Grandma that he didn't want a lot of fussing and changing with the plans. 'Either accept these blueprints as they are, my dear,' he said, 'or we won't build a house.' Grandma wasn't satisfied, but she recognized the mood, and the fact that there was nothing to be done about it. She approved the plans as Grandfather wished, and spent the next quarter century remodeling when he was busy with other concerns."

The Nova Scotia firm of Rhodes, Curry and Company won the construction tender and began work in the autumn of 1892. A year later, Alec and Mabel moved into their new home. It was a grand, rambling structure, with towers, big fireplaces, broad verandahs and sunny porches. Inside, the rooms were spacious but homey, well suited for the informal and relaxed family life that the Bells sought at Beinn Bhreagh. Mabel supervised the interior decoration: cherry and ash woodwork, walls painted in subdued colours and simple comfortable furniture.

Construction of Beinn Bhreagh Hall was just one of the projects Alec and Mabel undertook as they gradually transformed their property. The area

around the Hall became the hub of Beinn Bhreagh daily life. A gardener's cottage, sheep barns and paddocks were built just above the main house. Elsewhere there were homes for the farm workers, barns for the dairy cattle and horses and warehouses which held farm machinery, as well as Alec's experimental equipment and models.

Miles of roads crisscrossed the estate. The Hubbard Road, named for Mabel's parents, led up

Construction workers in front of Beinn Bhreagh Hall, completed in 1893.

Formal portrait of the Bells' elder daughter Elsie, painted in the late 1890s.

the mountain from the Lodge. The High Level Road followed the mountain side to Beinn Bhreagh Hall at the point. A winding mountain road ran from the Hall to the mountain top. It became known as Lovers Lane when Elsie Bell and her suitor Gilbert Grosvenor strolled along it in the summer of 1897. The Golden Wedding Road, named in 1894 to commemorate Alec's parents' 50th wedding anniversary, passed through the hardwood forest along the eastern shore of the headland. Gradually, the landscape and buildings of Beinn Bhreagh evolved to suit the needs of Alec and his family.

Freed from the constraints of a conventional working life by financial success, Alec was able to create his own way of life in which he could pursue his myriad interests. Beinn Bhreagh, however, provided not only ample facilities for his own experiments but also opportunity for Mabel to participate fully in community life and to develop a delightful home for a wide circle of family and friends.

2 Beinn Bhreagh:
The Life of a Family

Mabel Bell was at the centre of life at Beinn Bhreagh. "Everything begins with her," said her cousin Mary Blatchford, "and works around again to the same." She had been instrumental in the decision to create the family estate in Cape Breton and in many ways was more involved with its development and management than Alec. Mabel wanted to make Beinn Bhreagh an appropriate setting for Alec's scientific work, a place where he would continue to make significant contributions and a place that reflected his

Above: One of many prominent visitors to Beinn Bhreagh: Samuel P. Langley, secretary of the Smithsonian (left), relaxes in the sun porch with Alec, Daisy and Mabel. Right: The comfortable sitting room at Beinn Bhreagh—centre of family life.

status as a world-famous scientist. She also wanted Beinn Bhreagh to be central to a rich and enjoyable family life for her daughters and their children. "You who have lived together here, bound by common ties, can never in afterlife quite lose the affection and interest in each other which these visits foster," she wrote to Daisy's husband, David Fairchild.

Her firm belief that Beinn Bhreagh was first and foremost a family home meant that Mabel always ensured that the interests and hobbies of her family took precedence over running the property as a commercial farm. "Decorative effect and convenience and economy of labour," she admitted, "don't go together." From time to time, particularly when there were quarrels among the staff, Alec grew frustrated over the amount of time he and Mabel devoted to estate operations and would propose drastic changes, changes that would lessen the family's enjoyment of life there. He once declared, "Our chief concern with our Beinn Bhreagh property is financial"; to which Mabel replied bluntly that it was "*not* my *chief* concern." She argued, "We have other more interesting objects and I do not think our desire to have the place self-supporting will be allowed in the future any more than in the past to interfere with these other objects."

What is it? Three generations of the family share a moment of close observation.

So Mabel remained in overall control of the estate, working closely with a succession of farm managers and a staff of more than a dozen workmen.

Despite Alec's hopes, Beinn Bhreagh was not financially successful. It did, however, supply most of the daily needs of the family, crucial in the days before supermarkets and rapid transport of foodstuffs. The gardens produced a cornucopia of vegetables, from reliable staples such as potatoes, turnips and parsnips to the more exotic celery, eggplant and melons.

Raspberries, blackberries and other fruit flourished. Dairy cattle provided milk and butter; hens provided eggs; and pigs provided bacon and chops. The hay, oats and barley needed to feed all this livestock grew abundantly in the fields and pastures.

Beinn Bhreagh also provided a perfect setting for family summer activities. Sailing was a particular passion of Elsie's husband, Gilbert Grosvenor, and his family. His yacht, the *Elsie*, was built at Beinn Bhreagh and quickly became an important part of summer entertainment, taking part in regattas and races organized by local yacht clubs. Motor launches, among them the *Piper* and the *Kia Ora*, ferried the Bells, their family and guests on picnics and sightseeing trips around the lake. A series of houseboats took family members on overnight cruises. The first of these vessels, the *Mabel of Beinn Bhreagh*, was bought shortly after Alec and Mabel arrived in Baddeck and often carried the family around Bras d'Or Lake for week-long trips. Later it was beached on the east side of Beinn Bhreagh and became a favourite weekend retreat for Alec where, removed from the demands of sociability, he could let his inventive mind contemplate the myriad topics that interested him. Other houseboats followed: the *Ugly Duckling* and the *Getaway*, in which Alec and

Alec and Mabel in conversation in the motorboat *Ranzo* with the Lodge in the background.

Mabel, their daughters and several grandchildren cruised in 1914 when they set off on a camping trip up the nearby Washabuck River.

Mabel's activities were not confined to the estate. During the 30 years she spent at Baddeck, Mabel contributed to community life with both financial support to organizations and the influence of her prestigious name. Encouraged by Alec, her activities enabled her to make many friends within the village. Together, in 1891, they founded the Young Ladies Club of Baddeck, renamed the Bell Club in Alec's honour after his death. Using the model of women's clubs that Mabel had attended in Washington, the Baddeck club provided opportunities for its members to study and discuss issues of the day. The meetings ended sociably with good conversation and the more tangible delights of cake and tea. Mabel was its honorary president and cherished the companionship and friendships she formed, calling the club meetings some of her "dearest memories." Alec and Mabel also contributed to the development of a public library in Baddeck, with substantial donations of both money and books. In addition, Mabel funded the renovation of a building to house the library collection, naming it Gertrude Hall in honour of her mother.

A talented artist, Mabel had a lifelong interest in the visual arts. She was especially drawn to the arts and crafts movement of the 1890s. As much a philosophy as an art style, the movement advocated revival of traditional crafts that could give employment opportunities to people in rural areas, in particular to women. With these goals in mind, Mabel devoted considerable energy in the early years at

Members of the Young Ladies Club of Baddeck pose in costume following an evening program.

A free and easy life: Alec and Mabel's granddaughters Gertrude, Mabel and Lillian Grosvenor (r. to l.) out for a walk accompanied by their pet sheep.

Baddeck to developing a cottage industry based on the sale of handicrafts. She employed sewing teachers and searched for markets for the shirts, napkins and handkerchiefs that the women produced. When Governor General Lord Aberdeen and his wife visited Beinn Bhreagh in 1897, Mabel tried unsuccessfully to convince Lady Aberdeen, a keen supporter of women's causes, to take on sponsorship of the craft project. Interest in the project faded, but Daisy

Fairchild may have had her mother's work in mind when she encouraged development of the rug-hooking craft at Cheticamp many years later.

The new century brought joy and excitement to Beinn Bhreagh as the family circle expanded. Elsie and Daisy married men with broad interests and enquiring minds. Elsie's husband, Gilbert Grosvenor, was the son of a professor at Amherst College in Massachusetts and had been hired by Bell to be editor of the National Geographic Society's magazine. David Fairchild, who married Daisy in 1905, was a botanist with the American government who traveled around the world looking for new plant species that might benefit agriculture in the United States. In time, ten grandchildren arrived to provide new enjoyment and activity at Beinn Bhreagh.

These grandchildren frequently spent three or four months a year at Baddeck, especially during World War I. Alec and Mabel were enthusiastic and active grandparents and Beinn Bhreagh provided space and security for a free and adventurous life. Alec taught the children to swim, as he had taught their mothers, in a time-honoured way: a rope around the body and a quick jump off the wharf into the lake's cool waters. The children

Swimming lessons with Grandfather Alec.

The family with the new pony.

spent long days outside making pets of goats or lambs, riding the Shetland pony bought for them by their grandfather, and taking part in some of Alec's experiments. In the evenings, after family dinner, Alec contributed to their scientific education with simple but intriguing experiments that illustrated broader scientific principles. He demonstrated the principle of vacuums by showing how shelled hard-boiled eggs slipped inside a bottle when the air pressure inside was reduced by burning a candle to exhaust the oxygen. Or, he showed how air expands when it is heated by stretching a balloon over the neck of an empty bottle that was placed in a pot of hot water. The children watched in fascination as the balloon expanded as the air in the bottle warmed.

Mabel was also greatly interested in the education of children. As a young mother, she had searched unsuccessfully for a program of early childhood education to help her daughters develop to their full potential. The arrival of grandchildren rekindled her interest in pre-school education and it was with great curiosity that early in 1912 she visited a school run on the principles of the Italian educator, Dr. Maria Montessori. So impressed was she with the methods used—of encouraging the children to work independently and to learn through experimentation—that she arranged to have one of the Montessori teachers, Roberta Fletcher, come to Beinn Bhreagh to conduct a Montessori school for the Bell grandchildren. "I want my grandchildren to be workers and if the Montessori System does not make them efficient men and women, looking on work as the noblest thing of all, I shall be disappointed." Called the Children's

A casual family portrait at the Lodge, Gilbert Grosvenor on the left, Elsie on chair with Daisy and David Fairchild on the right.

Laboratory, the class was held in the upper storey of the old warehouse at Beinn Bhreagh: a big open room made pleasant and welcoming with child-sized chairs and tables, a piano and shelves filled with all kinds of objects for the children to study.

Mabel was pleased with the success of her summer experiment and sponsored a Montessori classroom at her home when she returned to Washington in the autumn. She played an active role in the establishment of the Montessori Educational Association, serving as its first president. When Dr. Montessori visited the United States in 1914, she paid tribute to Mabel Bell for her support. Mabel continued to advocate the Montessori methods, although interest in the movement soon waned, especially when the outbreak of World War I cut the movement off from its European roots and made it difficult to get trained teachers.

Life at Beinn Bhreagh followed a familiar routine for many years. Generally, Alec and Mabel arrived early in May and remained until late autumn, though they often stayed for longer periods, particularly when Alec was immersed in aviation experiments. During the summer, the estate was busy with a steady stream of family and friends, some of whom had their own summer homes in Baddeck, others who stayed at Beinn Bhreagh Hall for weeks at a time. The Grosvenors, with their six children, often spent at least three months at Beinn Bhreagh, using the old Lodge as their home. Daisy and David Fairchild and their three children stayed with the Bells at the Hall for a month or more each summer. Mabel delighted in marking special family occasions with lavish decorations. When the Fairchilds first visited Baddeck after their marriage they were greeted with bonfires on the mountainside, lanterns strung along the road to the Hall and rafts of burning sticks moored along the shore.

A highlight of the summer at Beinn Bhreagh was the Harvest Home celebrations, a grand event late in the summer to which all the estate workers and their families were invited. Athletic competitions were held on the fields along the shore, with men and boys taking part in tugs-of-war, hammer throwing and races. Prizes were awarded by the Bells and their guests, including Helen Keller when she visited Beinn Bhreagh in 1901. Then participants and spectators gathered in the old warehouse for a picnic feast of sandwiches, pies and cakes, followed by Scottish country dancing.

Top: Athletic contests at the Harvest Home celebrations in 1901. Above: Family and guests, including Helen Keller, on the porch at Beinn Bhreagh.

Women workers building dinghies for the Canadian navy during World War I.

Increasingly, Alec and Mabel spent much of the year in Baddeck, especially after the United States entered the war in 1917. Alec was busy with experiments on watercraft and with the boat-building contract that he hoped would lead to a major local industry. New sheds were built along the shore of Beinn Bhreagh Harbour and as more men left for war service, women were hired to replace them. Fourteen small lifeboat dinghies were constructed for the Canadian navy, but the contracts for larger ves-

Potatoes were planted on the lawns of Beinn Bhreagh as a contribution to the war effort.

sels did not follow. Mabel took an active role in community war projects, organizing sewing bees and fundraising concerts. She also tried her hand at methods of preserving food, especially non-traditional foods. The canned peas and corn that she prepared proved to be a success, and Alec reported that even the dried and powdered dandelion leaves could be boiled up to resemble finely chopped spinach. Mabel found great fulfillment in contributing to the war effort, telling Daisy, "We would be

Mabel inspecting udo plants, imported by David Fairchild and grown as an experiment at Beinn Bhreagh.

mere spectators in Washington; here we are doing something, not much, but more satisfying."

This involvement with the war effort work meant that the Bells were still at Beinn Bhreagh on December 6, 1917, when Halifax was devastated by the explosion of the munitions ship *Mont Blanc*. The concussion of the blast was felt at Baddeck and news soon came of the disaster. The community, like many in Nova Scotia, quickly organized to send help. Mabel immediately donated a shipment of blankets and winter clothing and Alec called for volunteers from his laboratory staff to go to Halifax to assist in the relief effort. Twelve men, led by foreman Walter Pinaud, set off on December 11 to catch the train at Grand Narrows en route to Halifax, where they worked for several weeks.

Family home, summer playground, self-sufficient farm: for 30 years, this was Beinn Bhreagh. Here the Bell family and friends enjoyed an active and memorable way of life presided over by Mabel Bell. But Beinn Bhreagh was even more—it was the scene of significant scientific achievements by Alec and his associates, achievements that connected his name to new and exciting technology.

3 "It will be all UP with us someday"

All his life Alec had been fascinated by flight. As a boy in Scotland he had watched birds circling above him and wondered how they were able to stay in the air. Even during his honeymoon, he pondered the possibilities of manned flight. Mabel was amazed at her new husband's inventiveness: "Flying machines to which telephones and torpedoes are to be attached occupy the first place just now from the observation of seagulls. Every now and then he comes back with another flying machine which has quite changed its shape within a quarter of an hour."

Other scientists and inventors shared this interest in manned flight. By 1891, Alec's friend Samuel Langley, secretary of the Smithsonian Institution, was experimenting with models of flying machines. Alec was enthusiastic: "I shall have to make experiments upon my own account in Cape Breton. Can't keep out of it. It will be all UP with us someday." The open fields of Beinn Bhreagh, the steady breezes off the lake and the availability of local workers made the Baddeck property a perfect place for Alec to pursue his experiments.

Alec was, however, a cautious man and well understood the risks inherent in experiments with manned flight. The safety of the pilot was his first concern. When the German flight experimenter Otto Lilienthal was killed in a glider accident in 1896, Alec knew his fears justified: "Accidents will happen, sooner or later, and the chances are largely in favour of the first accident being the last experiment." Alec concluded that self-propelled kites would prove to be the safest way of getting a man into the air.

Beginning in the 1890s, Alec experimented with a wide variety of kite designs. The people of Baddeck

One of Alec's experimental kites in front of the Beinn Bhreagh laboratory.

watched in fascination as huge three-wheeled kites, ring kites and box kites rose and fell over the meadows of Beinn Bhreagh. What was the point of all this—surely flying kites was for children! One bemused local observer noted, "He goes up there on the side of the hill on sunny afternoons and with a lot of thing-ma-jigs fools away the whole blessed day, flying kites, mind you. And the men that visit him—old men—that should have something better to do. They go up there with him and spend the whole livelong day fly-ing kites. It's the greatest foolishness I ever did see."

Alec (right) and his workers watching a large ring kite in flight.

Above: Conference at the laboratory - Alec and workers with a tetrahedral kite. Right: Casey Baldwin and laboratory workers demonstrating the strength of tetrahedral construction.

Keeping a cautious eye on the flight of a large tetrahedral kite.

Alec understood that what he needed was a light-weight yet strong framework large enough to carry a man into the air. In 1902 he realized that the shape he was looking for was a four-sided equilateral trian-gle: that is, a tetrahedron. The tetrahedron could not easily be bent out of shape and could be standard-ized for easy production. Covered with a light fabric, the cells could be joined together to form kites of many different shapes. Soon Alec's workers, includ-ing many women from the community, were mass-producing tetrahedral cells. Kite flying continued apace using the new design.

A family endeavour: (top) Melville Grosvenor dangles from a kite string and (above) Mabel measures the pull exerted by a kite.

Friends and family were pressed into service to help fly these experimental kites. Mabel tested their pull in flight; Helen Keller, with her keen sense of touch, noticed when the wire holding a kite was under too much stress and was likely to break. And Alec's oldest grandson Melville was everywhere: helping to launch the kites, hanging on to the kite wires and joining his grandfather and the workmen to haul the big ones safely back to earth.

In December 1905, Alec proved that kites could lift a man when the huge *Frost King* carried his workman Neil McDermid 30 feet into the air. Alec had insisted on staying at Beinn Bhreagh later than usual in hopes of getting winds strong enough to fly the big kite. As he always did, he took photographs of the experiment and was ecstatic when Mabel carefully developed the image that documented the achievement. The principle was confirmed two years later when the large *Cygnet* kite, towed by the steamer *Blue Hill*, carried a man on a seven-minute flight over the lake.

While Alec was preoccupied with kites, other experimenters were moving ahead with the more conventional biplane. The first successful manned flight was made without fanfare by Orville and Wilbur Wright in December 1903. Alec received news

of this success in 1905 when the Wrights' mentor
Octave Chanute attended a meeting at Bell's
Washington home. When asked what proof there
was that the Wrights had flown, Chanute replied, "I
have seen them do it." These simple words seized the
imagination of all those who, like Bell, were fascinated by the thought of heavier-than-air flight.

Mabel realized that Alec would benefit from
working with younger men who shared his enthusiasm about flight and had more technical training.
She encouraged Arthur McCurdy's son, Douglas, who
was studying engineering in Toronto, to bring a
friend home for the summer to help Alec in his aviation work. When Douglas returned to Baddeck in the

Top: Neil McDermid carried aloft by the *Frost King*. Above: The *Cygnet* on a barge under tow by the *Blue Hill.*

51

summer of 1906, he brought a young Ontario graduate in mechanical engineering, Frederick Walker Baldwin, always known as Casey. The choice proved perfect. Casey remained at Beinn Bhreagh for the rest of his life, working with Alec and becoming a close family friend.

Together Alec and Casey continued work on Alec's kites. They were joined the next year by Douglas McCurdy, now graduated, and by the young American army lieutenant Thomas Selfridge. He had a thorough knowledge of the theory of manned flight and was delighted with the chance to put his knowledge to practical purpose in Baddeck. Another young man joined the group in September 1907, Glenn Curtiss of Hammondsport, New York, already established as a manufacturer of motorcycles and lightweight but powerful aviation motors.

Together the four young men worked closely with Alec and brought a new spirit of enthusiasm and camaraderie to Beinn Bhreagh. After the workday was over, they gathered at the Hall for tea with Mabel and in the evenings they played billiards, talked of everything from sports to science, and sang cheerfully while Alec played the piano. They seemed almost like sons to Mabel: "My boys are all such good friends and yet so different, such jolly boys off duty, all so

full of fun and all so earnest when it's time for work."

Soon Mabel saw how she could help this new venture. She proposed that the men form an organization with the goal of getting a machine into the air and made the suggestion practical by volunteering $20,000 to fund the project. Alec in turn volunteered the use of his laboratory facilities. With his flair for the dramatic, Alec insisted that the five men travel to Halifax where their signatures on the formal agreement could be witnessed by the American consul. The new organization, called the Aerial Experiment Association, was to operate for one year.

The Aerial Experiment Association: (l. to r.) Glenn Curtiss, Casey Baldwin, Alexander Graham Bell, Tom Selfridge and Douglas McCurdy.

The *Red Wing* on the ice of Lake Keuka at Hammondsport before an experimental flight.

Shortly after its formation in October 1907, the group moved its base to Hammondsport to work during the winter, close to Curtiss' machine shop. Over the next year, the young men developed four flying machines, "aerodromes" as Bell thought they should be called. Gradually they achieved success. In March 1908, Casey flew the *Red Wing*, designed by

Tom Selfridge, for a short flight of 300 feet off the ice of Lake Keuka. A second flight was less successful when the craft crashed, fortunately without harm to its pilot. The second aerodrome was christened the *White Wing* and incorporated a number of design improvements, including hinged sections at the ends of the wings, called ailerons, which helped stabilize

Preparing the *White Wing* for a flight in Hammondsport.

Pilot Glenn Curtiss and the *June Bug*, before the record flight on July 4, 1908.

the craft. This time, the three men made several flights, one of more than 1000 feet, before the craft was badly damaged in a hard landing.

The success of the third craft, the *June Bug*, confirmed the AEA members as significant aviation experimenters. Late in June, Glenn Curtiss successfully flew the *June Bug* on a flight of nearly 3500 feet at an altitude of 20 feet. This success prompted the young men to challenge for the Scientific American trophy for the first flight of one kilometre. They wasted no time in preparing. The press was notified of the trial and on July 4 people gathered at Hammondsport to watch as Curtiss flew the *June Bug* more than 9000 feet, easily winning the trophy. Alec and Mabel were on their way back to Beinn Bhreagh but Daisy and David Fairchild witnessed the flight. Daisy immediately wrote to her parents, conveying the excitement of the occasion, "The actual sight of a man flying past me through the air was thrilling to a degree I can't express. We all lost our heads. David shouted and I cried, and everyone cheered and clapped, and engines hooted."

Curtiss flew the *June Bug* successfully several more times in July. Meanwhile work began on a fourth craft—Douglas McCurdy's *Silver Dart*, named because of its silver-coloured rubberized covering. Test flights of the *Dart* began early in December 1908. For the Aerial Experiment Association, however, the autumn of 1908 brought sadness when Tom Selfridge was killed on a test flight with Orville Wright. Selfridge's colleagues were stunned. Casey and Alec left Baddeck immediately for Washington to help investigate the cause of the crash.

Douglas McCurdy at the controls of the *Silver Dart* during its early trials at Hammondsport.

Mabel remained alone at Beinn Bhreagh remembering the young man who had endeared himself to everyone: "I miss the thought of him so much. Nobody ever did so many little things for me as he. Others have loved me more, of course, but he just saw the little things, pushing up my chair to the table or bringing a screen to shut off drafts, all so quietly and unobtrusively that no one noticed."

While in Washington, the surviving members of the AEA decided to extend the organization for another six months until March 1909. Mabel came to their aid with a commitment of a further $10,000. Curtiss and McCurdy returned to Hammondsport to continue work on the *Silver Dart* and made several successful flights before the craft was shipped to Baddeck for further testing.

On February 23, 1909, the *Silver Dart* was ready for its first test in Canada. The day was cold and clear. News of the trial spread through the village—school children and adults, all keen to witness the event, thronged Baddeck Bay. The *Silver Dart*, piloted by Douglas McCurdy, was towed out on the ice. The first attempt had to be halted when a fuel line broke. Repairs were quickly made. The motor was restarted and the *Silver Dart* began to move forward. Then the

boys skating alongside were left behind as the fragile craft rose into the air and flew above the ice for about a half mile at a speed of 40 mph, the fastest any AEA machine had flown.

It was a historic achievement—the first flight of a heavier-than-air machine in Canada. Mabel, like the other spectators, was keen for a second test, but Alec was determined not to mar the occasion by risking an unsuccessful flight. Instead, spectators and experimenters alike were invited back to the old warehouse on the Beinn Bhreagh shore where sandwiches and hot drinks were waiting for the celebration of such a momentous event.

Top: The *Silver Dart* towed by horse and sleigh. Above: Douglas McCurdy and the *Silver Dart* soar above the Beinn Bhreagh shoreline.

The Aerial Experiment Association had succeeded in its aims. They had done more than just "get into the air." Casey Baldwin had become the first Canadian to fly and Douglas McCurdy in the *Silver Dart* had made the first flight in Canada. Now it was over. On March 31, 1909, Alec, Douglas and Casey met at Beinn Bhreagh Hall to wind up the association. They passed a resolution thanking Mabel for her help and expressing their "highest appreciation of her loving and sympathetic devotion without which the work of the Association would have come to naught." At midnight, the Association ended.

Aviation experiments still preoccupied Casey and Douglas. Alec provided financial backing for them to establish the Canadian Aerodrome Company, which would build aircraft for sale. They set up shop in the old Kite House, hired as foreman a mechanic who had worked on the Silver Dart, and employed a staff of about ten workmen. The company built two aircraft, prosaically named *Baddeck No. 1* and *Baddeck No. 2*, as well as a monoplane commissioned by Mabel's cousin Gardiner Greene Hubbard III. After both the *Silver Dart* and *Baddeck No. 1* crashed during test flights at the Canadian military base in Petawawa, Ontario, in August 1909, Casey and Douglas spent

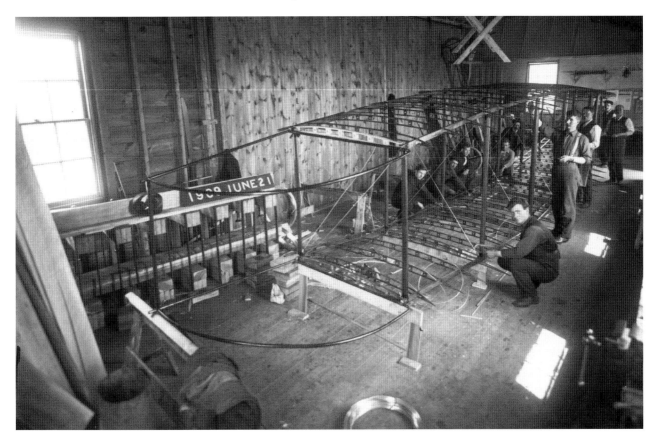

Canadian Aerodrome Company workers assembling the wing of the *Baddeck*.

the autumn testing the *Baddeck No. 2* at their new landing strip on a field in Big Baddeck Valley.

Alec had the houseboat *Ugly Duckling* towed up the Baddeck River to the landing field and regularly camped on board, observing the flights and joining in discussions with the young men on how the machines could be improved. Mabel frequently drove over from Beinn Bhreagh with her guests to picnic and watch the progress of the flights. Test

AEA members experimenting with a glider in their progress towards successful flight.

flights continued on Baddeck Bay in the new year when the ice was strong enough. Support from the Canadian government to continue the development of the aircraft was not forthcoming, however, and experiments ceased when Casey and his wife Kathleen left Baddeck in April 1910 to join the Bells on a world tour. Douglas McCurdy also left Baddeck and later joined Glenn Curtiss' aviation company in the United States. Advances in aviation continued elsewhere, but Baddeck's fame as the site of that first historic flight, and the fame of the members of the Aerial Experiment Association as significant aviation pioneers, were enduring.

4 Boats That Fly

Among the ideas that Alec and his young associates had considered while they were experimenting with flying machines was the use of hydrofoils, or hydroplanes as they called them, to enable aircraft to take off and land on water. Alec's concern as always was for safety and he thought that water take-off would be a boon for aviators. A keen sailor, Casey was also interested in designing faster boats by developing technology that would lift the boat's hull clear of the water to lessen resistance. They experimented

Above: Alec helping to launch wheeled floats used in early experiments on hydrofoils. Right: Alec and workman Hector McNeil with two models of hydrofoil designs.

with a variety of designs, but it was not until Alec and Casey returned from their world tour that they began serious consideration of the use of hydrofoils. During their tour, they had stopped at Milan to visit the Italian engineer Forlanini who had already built a vessel using hydrofoils. Back in Beinn Bhreagh in August 1911, they discussed possible designs for a similar vessel and together they set to work.

Models and towing experiments occupied their attention at first. Tin models were constructed by Hector McNeil, a meticulous and inventive work-man who had worked with Alec for many years, both in Washington and Baddeck. The models were equipped with hydrofoils in a variety of designs, most with slats, similar to ladders. The Beinn Bhreagh motorboats towed the models along marked courses both within Beinn Bhreagh Harbour and on the open waters of Baddeck Bay. Alec and Casey watched intently, making notes on the per-formance of the craft, how well they lifted out of the water and what speed was reached. During the evening conferences that had become a ritual for them, the two men reviewed the results, discussing what the day's trials had taught them and what changes could be made.

In the meantime, work started on the full-sized craft that Casey had designed. By November 1911, the vessel—nearly 30 feet long with a 50-horsepower engine—was ready for testing. The hydrodrome, as Casey called it, was named *HD-1* and carried two of Alec's workmen: William McDonald at the helm and Kenneth Ingraham tending the engine. On its second day of tests it reached a speed of 30 mph. Alec and Mabel had already returned to Washington but both were excited when Casey sent news of the success. Alec immediately telegraphed, "30 m.p.h. is splendid beginning. Big congratulations. Hope for 50 soon." His hopes were not realized, although the *HD-1* did achieve a speed of 40 mph before ice stopped the trials.

The next summer saw more success with the *HD-1*. By August Alec and Casey were confident enough to take passengers aboard. Casey's wife Kathleen and Elsie Grosvenor were among those who went out for a ride on Baddeck Bay. Always adventurous, Mabel was keen to take her turn, but the ever-cautious Alec decreed that no non-swimmers should risk a trip on a craft that was still experimental. His caution was justified in October when the floats were badly damaged and the vessel

had to be towed back to shore. Repaired and renamed the *HD-2*, or the *Jonah*, since it had risen from the depths, it made several trials late in November before winter brought an end to the experiments.

Workmen preparing the *HD-1* for a test run, 1912.

Stern view of the *HD-3* on the slip outside the boatshed.

While the Bells spent the winter months in Washington, Casey designed the *HD-3*, slightly smaller but incorporating changes based on the experience gained from the *HD-1* and *HD-2*. It made several test runs in August 1913, including one that was witnessed by the Prince of Monaco who visited Baddeck as part of a cruise through Bras d'Or Lakes on his yacht, *Hirondelle*. Unfortunately, during the run the propeller was damaged. Repairs were completed late in the fall, but again winter ended further testing.

The outbreak of war in August 1914 brought abrupt changes to experimental work at Beinn Bhreagh. Alec had become an American citizen many years earlier. Since the United States had not declared war on Germany, he found himself a citizen of a neutral country. As such, he thought that it was not honourable to undertake any work that might assist one of the warring countries. From the early days of experiments with hydrofoils, Alec thought that they would prove effective against submarines, already an important weapon. Consequently, all work on the hydrodromes ceased and the Bells concentrated on contributing to the war effort within the community.

In April 1917, the United States declared war against Germany. Alec had expected the declaration and had already resumed some experiments with hydrofoils during the winter, when he and Mabel had stayed with the Fairchilds in their Florida home. With the United States at war, he was free to respond to the American navy's call for fast submarine

Alec and Mabel on the wharf at Beinn Bheagh after a successful test of the *HD-4*.

chasers. He immediately returned to Beinn Bhreagh to begin work with Casey. Mabel wanted to make a significant contribution to this war effort and offered to fund construction of a hydrofoil craft. Alec and Casey helped by offering their services free of charge.

Casey's new craft, named the *HD-4*, benefited from the knowledge gained during the earlier experiments. It was much larger, at 60 feet long, and cylindrical in shape. Casey nicknamed it the *Cigar*. It was constructed at the Beinn Bhreagh boatyard during 1917, but, because the powerful engines promised by the American navy did not arrive until July 1918, the *HD-4* was not launched until that October.

Trials were soon underway and gradually adjustments were made to improve performance. The people of Baddeck became used to the noise of the unmuffled engines as the craft roared along the measured courses set up on the lake. By late December, the craft had achieved a maximum speed of nearly 54 mph. As usual, Mabel often took part in discussions between Casey and Alec and eagerly watched the trials. At last, on November 13, she achieved her ambition to ride in a hydrofoil craft. She took part in a short speed trial on the quarter-mile course and then enjoyed a longer excursion over

to Baddeck. Alec, who never rode in the *HD-4*,
watched intently from the wharf until Mabel was
safely back on dry land at Beinn Bhreagh.

 Although the war ended on November 11, Alec
and Casey continued their work on the *HD-4* to
prove that a hydrofoil craft would have a valuable
role to play in naval operations. Experiments ended
early in January when ice in the lake became too
thick for safe tests. Alec reported their success to both
American and Canadian naval authorities and asked
for the loan of more powerful engines to continue
speed trials. The American navy responded by

Alec watching the *HD-4* with Mabel on board.

The *HD-4* thunders past at high speed.

shipping two 350-hp Liberty engines to Baddeck the next summer. On September 9, 1919, the new engines proved their worth when the *HD-4* reached a speed of 70.86 mph over a one-mile course in Baddeck Bay, setting a record for watercraft. Many spectators shared the excitement of the day and Alec promptly announced the success to the press. Newspapers as far afield as Washington and London reported the event. It was indeed an accomplishment, especially for private individuals working with only minimal government support.

Alec still hoped to interest the American and Canadian governments in the craft and issued invitations to naval officers from both countries to come to Baddeck to observe the trials. The only response was the visit of a lieutenant from the fledging Canadian navy who arrived in October 1918 and was taken out for a run in the *HD-4*. The publicity arising from the record-setting run in 1919 had more effect. In the summer of 1920, officers from both the Royal Navy and the American navy arranged inspection tours to Beinn Bhreagh. Three officers from the British Admiralty spent most of July in Baddeck observing the *HD-4* in a variety of weather conditions and carrying loads of differing weights. The officers, including Commander C.C. "Tommy" Dobson, winner of the Victoria Cross for his bravery during a naval attack in 1919, added a touch of glamour to the usual summer activities at Beinn Bhreagh, joining eagerly in sailing, tennis and picnics. The visit also sparked romance between the young Commander Dobson and Mabel's secretary, Polly MacMechan. They were married later that autumn in England. The visit of the American officers in September was more hurried and much less social. They spent a bare 48 hours at Beinn Bhreagh closely observing the *HD-4* as it was put through its

Alec posing in the cockpit of the *HD-4*.

The *HD-4* beached on the shore at Beinn Bhreagh below the Lodge, 1956.

paces by Alec's assistant, Sydney Breeze, left in charge when Casey set off for England on the yacht *Typhoon*.

Reports prepared by both groups of observers concluded that the *HD-4* was a significant scientific achievement. The British Admiralty went so far as to request Alec and Casey to submit a quote for construction of a similar hydrofoil craft. However, changing naval priorities early in the 1920s brought an end to this project. The record-setting *HD-4* was stripped of its engines and hauled up on the rocky beach below the Lodge where it remained, alone and decrepit, until 1957, when it was moved across Baddeck Bay to the newly opened Bell Museum.

5 "Go on inventing"

Addressing a meeting of inventors in 1891, Alec declared, "Wherever you may find the inventor, you may give him wealth or you may take away from him all that he has; and he will go on inventing. He can no more help inventing than he can help thinking or breathing." Alec's life exemplified this commitment to science and discovery. His endless curiosity led him to investigate a wide variety of issues, from aviation to hydrofoils, to one of the first x-ray photographs taken in Canada. He

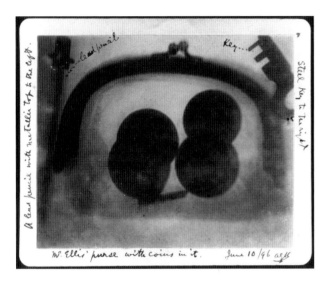

Coins in a change purse, possibly the first x-ray photo taken in Canada, 1896.

undertook exhaustive studies of the inheritance of deafness and of longevity. Genetics was the basis of his longest-running experiment: 32 years of sheep breeding at Beinn Bhreagh. The study started in 1889 when Alec purchased the farmland on Red Head. One farm came with a flock of sheep and Alec soon began to wonder why sheep regularly produced single lambs rather than twins. To have twin lambs, he thought, would help the sheep-farmers of Cape Breton by making their livelihood more profitable.

Alec set about developing a strain of sheep that would consistently give birth to twins. He thought that twin-bearing might be more common in sheep that had more than the usual two nipples. In time he established a flock composed of sheep with four, six and more nipples, but consistent twin production remained elusive. As usual, he kept meticulous records: individual sheep were identified with a system of earmarks that he developed and gradually pedigrees of many generations were compiled and studied.

Early in the 20th century, Alec began to investigate environmental factors that might affect twin production, such as nutrition and time of breeding. The sheep were brought down from their shelters in "Sheepville" at the top of Beinn Bhreagh Mountain

Top: Sheep from Alec's experimental flock on the hill below Beinn Bhreagh Hall. Left: Alec feeding sheep, 1894.

to the Point where they could easily be monitored. The farm manager, John Davidson, designed and built a new barn with individual feeding stalls and a weighing box so that detailed records of diet and weight for each sheep could be kept. When it seemed that good nutrition was important for twin production, Alec had a glassed-in nursery added to the barn so that the lambs, now born early in March, could be housed in warm shelter for their first months.

Davidson left Beinn Bhreagh in 1914 to settle on his own farm near Halifax. Alec gave him most of the flock and auctioned the rest. Mabel, however, was convinced that her husband would miss this long-lasting experiment and bought some of the sheep back. Thereafter, Alec always referred to them as "Mrs. Bell's flock," but it was he who continued to manage all aspects of their care and to maintain the exhaustive records. His last scientific observations before his death was an analysis of the flock in which he concluded that it was indeed a true twin-breeding stock. Later studies by professional geneticists disputed this conclusion, suggesting instead that the high number of twins was due to the excellent feed and personalized attention that Alec and his workers had lavished on the sheep.

Alec's 30 years of sheep breeding reflected not only his scientific curiosity but also his concern to contribute to society. He defined an inventor as someone who "looks around the world, and is not contented with things as they are. He wants to improve what he sees, he wants to benefit the world." One problem he frequently considered was the plight of shipwrecked mariners who died of dehydration while surrounded by miles of ocean. He came up with a range of proposals, including waveactuated bellows that blew moist air into submerged bottles where it could condense. One summer he and the manager of the Beinn Bhreagh laboratory spent hours reading while they breathed into long glass tubes that condensed water from the breath. Water was indeed produced but since both men were smokers the taste left much to be desired. Nonetheless, Alec was convinced that condensation could provide water in an emergency and insisted that Casey take distilling equipment on board his yacht *Typhoon* for the journey to England in 1920.

Late in his life Alec's experiments in obtaining fresh water from salt had a more practical trial at Beinn Bhreagh. When the water supply to the house was found to be unsafe for drinking, he set up a

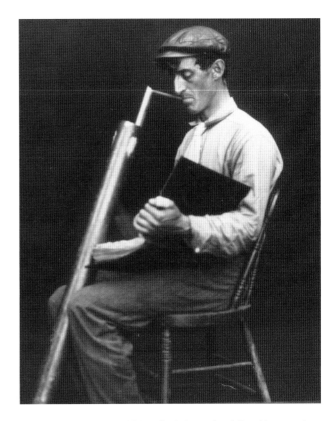

Laboratory supervisor William Bedwin reads while taking part in a condensation experiment.

79

"The work of the devil": Alec's vacuum jacket in use to resuscitate a sheep.

series of solar stills based on a design he had developed. They were shallow boxes with sloping glass covers into which a dish of salt water was placed. Fresh water condensed on the glass as the sun heated the salt water. Together the stills provided enough water to supply the family's needs.

Personal sadness was the impetus for another invention that Alec hoped would benefit society. Following the death of his premature son in 1881, he developed an artificial breathing apparatus that he called a vacuum jacket. It was an airtight cylinder that was placed around the chest. When air was pumped out a partial vacuum was created causing the chest to expand and air to be sucked into the lungs. In the 1890s, Alec and Daisy conducted experiments with the jacket at Beinn Bhreagh and were able to revive a sheep that had been drowned in the name of science. This return to life was too much for one of Alec's workmen who complained that it was clearly the work of the devil and promptly quit his job, refusing even to accept the pay he was owed. Although Alec hoped that the jacket would help drowning victims it was not much of an improvement over conventional methods of artificial respiration. The principle, however,

Alec and Mabel's daughters, Elsie (left) and Daisy (right), donated thousands of models and artifacts to form the Alexander Graham Bell Museum at Baddeck.

was the basis of the iron lung, developed independently in the 1920s to help polio patients.

After this successful trial, the vacuum jacket was safely stored away. Gradually, hundreds of objects—reminders of past experiments, successful and unsuccessful—began to accumulate at Beinn Bhreagh. Models of flying machines, some whimsical and some practical, models of hydrofoil craft, products of Hector McNeil's precise workmanship, propellers in all shapes and sizes, all were stored in the old Kite House, carefully dated and preserved. There they remained as mementos of a long and active life until 1954 when they were donated to the Bell Museum by Alec and Mabel's daughters.

6 "Gladly I lived"

For 30 years, daily life at Beinn Bhreagh revolved around Alec and his scientific work. He rose late, long after the rest of the household was up, and dictated an account of the previous day's activities to his secretary. David Fairchild thought that this practice gave Alec the pleasure of living his life twice. By midday Alec was at work in his office either in the Laboratory or the Kite House. He took part in whatever experiments were underway, discussing problems and solutions with Casey and the other workers

Alec and Mabel returning to Beinn Bhreagh Hall along a woodland path.

and writing up the results of their work. Mabel arrived late in the afternoon and together they walked back to the Hall deep in conversation all the while. In the evenings Alec often played the piano for family singsongs. Then, after the others had gone off to bed, he settled down in solitude to read and think, continuing his lifelong practice of working far into the night. As a young woman, Mabel had poked gentle fun at his habits by painting his portrait depicting him as a night owl, but as the years passed she had become resigned to his habits.

Inexorably this pattern of life was approaching an end. In 1914, Alec, then 67, was diagnosed with diabetes. The only treatment possible in the days before insulin was strict adherence to diet, a difficult prescription for a man who enjoyed food. He remained active and busy with projects, but Mabel was aware that the family life she had created and cherished was drawing to a close. She encouraged her grandchildren to spend as much time as possible with Alec. In 1917, as Beinn Bhreagh hummed with projects for war relief and hydrofoil trials, she urged David Fairchild to send his scientifically minded son Sandy to Baddeck for the summer: "He will be in surroundings and subject to influences that never again can be his. Daddysan, up to quite lately, has been remarkable well, and I hope he will be so again. I want your gifted boy to know him while he is still bright and full of mental vigor, and he has been so to an unusual degree this summer."

In the autumn of 1920, Alec and Mabel made their last visit to Britain. While there, Alec was granted the freedom of the city of Edinburgh, where he had been born more than 70 years earlier. Many other honours had come to him since he had left Britain as a sickly youth in 1870. He had been awarded 12 honorary

The night owl: Mabel's portrait of Alec, 1876.

The Volta Bureau, constructed in 1893 in Washington to hold documents relating to Alec's study of deafness.

degrees and had won prize medals from many technological organizations, including the prestigious Volta Prize for scientific achievement awarded by the French government, and the Thomas Alva Edison Medal from the American Institute of Electrical Engineers. He was renowned for his support of public education for deaf children and to the end of his life proclaimed that recognition of this work was "more pleasing to me than even recognition of my work with the telephone."

Alec and Mabel took an extended trip to the Caribbean during the winter of 1922. They enjoyed themselves immensely, trying new experiences and seeing new sights. Mabel, still adventurous, donned a full diving suit to go underwater and Alec entered an underwater chamber to observe tropical fish. Alec's growing weakness was, however, becoming clear. Back in Beinn Bhreagh in June, the cool fresh air seemed to revive him. He watched trials of a model of the hydrofoil target that Casey had designed for naval gunnery practice. He inspected the lambs born that spring and carefully reviewed their pedigrees. He drafted an article summarizing the breeding experiments, intending to prepare it for publication.

Then at the end of July his health abruptly deteriorated. He remained semi-conscious for a few

days, rallying occasionally to dictate a last tribute to the loving family life that had been the bedrock of his existence: "Mrs. Bell and I have both had a very happy life together, and we couldn't have had better daughters than Elsie and Daisy or better sons-in-law than Bert and David and we couldn't have had finer grandchildren."

Alec watching as Mabel is helped into a diving suit on a Caribbean holiday in 1922.

Family and friends at Alec's funeral on the mountain top at Beinn Bhreagh, August 4, 1922.

Alec died early in the morning of August 2, 1922, as he lay peacefully in his sleeping porch, open to the cool night air that he relished. Mabel stood beside him, her hand in his. For 45 years, they had shared life together. Daisy, who had arrived a few days earlier, described her mother's loss to Elsie, travelling in South America, "You never forget for a moment that the heart of everything has gone out of life for her forever."

Alec had told Mabel many years earlier that he wanted to be buried at the top of Beinn Bhreagh Mountain. Now she planned his funeral with care and dignity. The grave was prepared beside the tall tower that Casey had built with Alec's tetrahedral cells as his first project at Beinn Bheagh. A simple pine coffin was made by Alec's workers at the Laboratory and his grandchildren solemnly sewed fir branches on a pall of linen. The day of the funeral was gray and misty, the sort of weather Alec had always enjoyed. His coffin was carried to the mountaintop on a horse-drawn wagon, followed on foot by a procession of the men who had worked closely with Alec for years and accompanied by a car bearing Mabel, Daisy and the children, driven by Catherine MacKenzie, Alec's last secretary.

Top: Alec's gravestone, bearing the simple statement "inventor, teacher, died a citizen of the U.S.A." Above: The tetrahedral tower on opening day, August 31, 1907. Mabel had it demolished following Alec's death rather than letting it deteriorate.

The service at the mountaintop was plain and unpretentious. Local musician Jean MacDonald sang several old airs, including Robert Louis Stevenson's requiem, "Gladly I lived and gladly I die, and I lay me down with a will." The Reverend John MacKinnon read Longfellow's "A Psalm of Life," whose verses Mabel thought exemplified Alec's philosophy: "Let us, then, be up and doing, / With a heart for any fate; / Still achieving, still pursuing, / Learn to labor and to wait." A simple funeral, Alec's cousin Charles Bell called it, but Daisy thought how appropriate it was, "like a last message from Daddysan."

In the weeks that followed, Mabel was surrounded by friends and family, enjoying all the usual summer activities of Beinn Bhreagh. She joined the family on sailing excursions and organized picnics and exploring trips in the countryside. Her thoughts, however, were centred on safeguarding Alec's legacy. She was particularly concerned to fulfill Alec's wish that the scientific work that he and Casey had begun would be continued and that Casey and his family could remain in their home at Beinn Bhreagh. With this duty in mind, she drew up an agreement to fund Casey's experiments for 10 years. As well, she pondered

Mabel working at her desk in Beinn Bhreagh following Alec's death.

the future of the sheep flock, not wanting to waste Alec's years of study. She carried on Alec's plans in hopes of finding a farmer who would continue with the experimental flock in the future. Of greatest concern to her, though, was Alec's biography. She wanted a book that would portray the full breadth of his character, "broad-minded, generous and tolerant in some things beyond the comprehension of most and

"A very happy life together": Alec and Mabel, Beinn Bhreagh.

then curiously the opposite in others." Her son-in-law Gilbert Grosvenor, editor of the National Geographic Society's magazine, suggested the famous English writer, Lytton Strachey, but Mabel was not prepared to rush into a decision: "It would look as if we thought Father's fame ephemeral and wanted to get all there was out of it." Alec's papers and notebooks were carefully preserved but no work began on a biography.

Elsie kept her mother company at Beinn Bhreagh as the autumn months passed. Gradually, she realized that Mabel's health was also failing and persuaded her to return to Washington for medical care. Early in January 1923, Mabel Bell died at Daisy's Maryland home. Her ashes were interred in Alec's grave at the top of Beinn Bhreagh Mountain on August 7. Following her wishes, the time chosen was 5:00 p.m., the hour when for years she had joined Alec at the Laboratory to bring him home to the family.

The evening routine: Mabel arrives at the laboratory to accompany Alec on his walk home to Beinn Bhreagh Hall, 1909.

Sites

Bibliography

Canada Science and Technology Museum

Part of the National Museums of Canada network and includes the Canadian Aviation Museum, which houses the 1959 *Silver Dart* replica.

1867 St Laurent Boulevard
Ottawa, Ontario K1G 5A3

Telephone: 613-991-3044
Toll free: 1-866-442-4416
TTY: 613-991-9207

Email: cts@technomuses.ca
www.sciencetech.technomuses.ca

Canadian Aviation Museum

11 Aviation Parkway

Ottawa, Ontario K1K 4R3

Telephone: 613-993-2010
Toll free: 1-800-463-2038

www.aviation.technomuses.ca

Alexander Graham Bell National Historic Site of Canada

Chebucto Street (Route 205), P.O. Box 159
Baddeck, Nova Scotia B0E 1B0

Telephone: 902-295-2069
Fax: 902-295-3496

Email: information@pc.gc.ca
www.pc.gc.ca/lhn-nhs/ns/grahambell/index_e.asp

Bell Homestead National Historic Site of Canada

94 Tutela Heights Road
Brantford, Ontario N3T 1A1

Telephone: 519-756-6220
Fax: 519-759-5975

Email: Brian Wood, Curator, bwood@brantford.ca
          Sarah Hamilton, Education Co-ordinator,
          shamilton@brantford.ca

www.bellhomestead.on.ca

Bruce, Robert V. *Bell: Alexander Graham Bell and the Conquest of Solitude*. Little, Brown: New York, 1973.

MacKenzie, Catherine. *Alexander Graham Bell: The Man who Contracted Space*. Houghton Mifflin: Boston and New York, 1928.

Parkin, J.H. *Bell and Baldwin: Their Development of Aerodromes and Hydrodromes at Baddeck, Nova Scotia*. University of Toronto Press: Toronto, 1964.

Alexander Graham Bell Papers, Alexander Graham Bell National Historic Site of Canada, Baddeck.

Index